FROM:

DATE:

STAND
&
BE
COUNTED

WHITE STONE BOOKS
LAKELAND, FLORIDA

Unless otherwise indicated, all scripture quotations are taken from the *Holy Bible, New International Version*®. NIV®. Copyright © 1973, 1978, 1984 by International Bible Society. Used by permission of Zondervan Publishing House. All rights reserved.

Scripture quotations marked NLT are taken from the *Holy Bible, New Living Translation,* copyright © 1996. Used by permission of Tyndale House Publishers, Inc., Wheaton, Illinois 60189. All rights reserved.

Verses marked TLB are taken from *The Living Bible* © 1971. Used by permission of Tyndale House Publishers, Inc., Wheaton, Illinois 60189. All rights reserved.

07 06 05 04   10 9 8 7 6 5 4 3 2 1

Stand and Be Counted
Discover the Difference One Vote Can Make
ISBN 1-59379-030-9
Copyright © 2004 by White Stone Books, Inc.
P.O. Box 2835
Lakeland, Florida 33806

Printed in the United States of America. All rights reserved under International Copyright Law. Contents and/or cover may not be reproduced in whole or in part in any form without the express written consent of the Publisher.

INTRODUCTION

Once while debating a prominent political observer on CNN, I was asked about the separation of church and state. The host seemed upset that Christians were getting involved in politics. I reminded him the constitution does not even contain the phrase, "separation of church and state," and that our Founding Fathers were dedicated Christians who used the Bible to develop our constitution. Sadly, my words landed on deaf ears. But I pray this book will help you understand the believer's role in America today.

Our country was founded on principles found in the Bible, and today more than ever, we need to pray for our country and get involved in the democratic process—just like the early Americans. The Bible says faith without works is dead, so this book contains both prayers, written by pastor and author Michael Klassen, and dozens of ways to get educated and take action. My prayer is that you'll use this book to help restore America.

Thomas M. Freiling

"Let us resolve to be masters, not the victims, of our history—controlling our own destiny without giving way to blind suspicions and emotions."

—JOHN F. KENNEDY

REGISTER TO VOTE

Many of us—more than 50 millions citizens in this country—are eligible to vote but don't even bother to register. If you are at least 18 years old, you may register to vote. In all but four states you must register before Election Day, and in many states you must register 30 days before an election.

Don't wait! Registering to vote is easy. For the first time in American history, there is a national voter registration form. This means anyone can register from anywhere. Visit **http://www.fec.gov/votregis/vr.htm** to download the National Mail Voter Registration Form. You can make copies of this form and distribute them in your church, neighborhood, and to family and friends.

DID YOU KNOW?

The US Presidential candidate with the highest popular vote ever was Ronald Reagan. In 1984 he secured 54,455,075 votes. Reagan was also the candidate with the highest electoral vote: 525, in 1984. In that year he equalled the 49 states that Nixon carried in 1972.

A proclamation was then issued throughout Judah and Jerusalem for all the exiles to assemble in Jerusalem. Anyone who failed to appear within three days would forfeit all his property, in accordance with the decision of the officials and elders, and would himself be expelled from the assembly of the exiles.

EZRA 10:7-8

A PRAYER FOR HIGH VOTER TURNOUT

Almighty God,

As we approach Election Day, we ask that you would stir the hearts of the American people.

Awaken us from our complacency so we will take the upcoming election seriously and vote. May we witness an extraordinary turnout at the polls so that the candidates elected and issues passed will truly represent the American people and not special interests.

Pull us out of our individualistic mindset that assumes every person is autonomous. And build within our nation a sense of community so that everyone will see that he or she is playing a part in the decision-making process through the candidates we elect and the issues we approve.

All too often, we lose heart in the election process because we believe our vote won't make a difference. Remind us of the 2000 Presidential Election when every vote *did* count. May we not regret in the future our complacencies of the past.

On Election Day, renew our confidence in the election process. Please remind us that You can take the chaos of election day to assert Your will. For this reason we refuse to place our trust in the election. We place our trust in You.

Amen.

Scripture references:

Judges 21:5-6;
Amos 6:1;
1 Corinthians 1:10

ANSWER TELEPHONE SURVEYS

From time to time you may receive a telephone call from a pollster. We are all bothered by telemarketers, and many of us hang up without even listening. But if you want your voice to be heard you should politely listen and give your honest feedback. Why? Most polls are samplings of a very small population. Some national poll results you read about in newspapers are samplings of less than 1,000 voters.

So even though you are only one person, your answers could have nationwide impact. These polls are often touted by candidates and in the news media to sway voters. So the next time you get a phone call asking you to give your opinion on a candidate or issue, stand up and make a difference!

STAND AND BE COUNTED
★ ★ ★

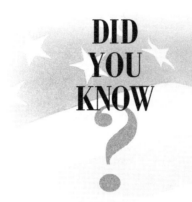

In 1800, John Adams and Thomas Jefferson ran against each other for President. The election was so close, the House of Representatives couldn't even decide after 35 votes. On the 36th vote, the House finally voted for Aaron Burr as an alternative, but the Supreme Court demanded a state by state vote, which resulted in Thomas Jefferson as the country's third President.

*Oh, the depth of the riches both of the
wisdom and knowledge of God!
how unsearchable are his judgments,
and his ways past, finding out! For
who hath known the mind of the Lord?
or who hath been his counselor?
Or who hath first given to him, and it
shall be recompensed unto him again?"
For of him, and through him, are all things:
To whom be glory forever. Amen.*

ROMANS 11:33-36 KJV

A PRAYER FOR DECLARING GOD'S DOMINION OVER THE ELECTION

God of heaven and earth,
With confidence I proclaim Your
unparalleled dominion over all the

nations of the earth including the United States of America. From Your holy throne you rule over our nation and by Your hand You raise up our leaders and take them down. "The king's heart is like a stream of water directed by the LORD; he turns it wherever he pleases."

Your power extends over the legislatures, judicial courts, national affairs, daily events, even the trivial nuances of my life. You were there before the foundations of our country were laid and Your power continues throughout eternity. You are stronger than any President, wiser than any judge, and greater than my heart.

Not even the powers of darkness can overcome the light of Your glory. And at the end of the age "every knee will bow in heaven and on earth and under the earth, and every tongue confess that Jesus is Lord to the glory of God the Father."

Because You are in complete control, I don't need to fear the outcome of the upcoming elections. Because You are greater than our hearts, You know everything. Despite our misguided zeal, our ill-informed decisions and our personal agendas, we know that You work out everything in conformity with the purpose of Your will. Thank You that our fate doesn't lie solely in the ballot box. Through my prayers I choose to join You in Your work.

Amen.

Scripture references:

Psalm 33:4, 47:8, 139:6, 147:5; Proverbs 21:1 (NLT); Job 38:4; Isaiah 55:9; Daniel 4:37; Matthew 6:10; Ephesians 1:11; Philippians 2:9-11 (NIV); 1 John 3:20

SIGN AN ONLINE PETITION

One fast and effective way to make a difference is to join other like-minded citizens by signing an online petition. At **www.grassfire.org** and **www.reclaimamerica.org,** you can sign a petition and forward it to your friends and family. You get to see how many friends follow your lead and how many "e-generations" your message travels.

Technology makes it possible for millions of people to be heard by our judges and lawmakers. One recent petition prompted more than 50,000 telephone calls to the office of a prominent United States Senator who was soon to vote on pro-life legislation. Think you're just one voice? Think again!

*"Truth is...
the best vindication
against slander."*

—ABRAHAM LINCOLN

These are the things you are to do:
Speak the truth to each other,
and render true and sound judgment
in your courts; do not plot evil
against your neighbor, and
do not love to swear falsely.

ZECHARIAH 8:16-17

A PRAYER FOR CAMPAIGNS GROUNDED IN TRUTH

Dear Almighty God,

All of us wrestle with the temptation to make ourselves appear better than we really are: to tell people what they want to hear. To make promises we know we cannot keep. To point out the faults in others over the faults of our own. And in reality, election campaigns only reflect what lies in every heart.

But You are the God who sees all, the God who knows us better than we know ourselves. You aren't impressed with our words, credentials, or experience because You look at our hearts.

Your word tells us that out of the abundance of the heart the mouth speaks. Please reveal what resides within the candidates' hearts. Bring clarity to their words and help them avoid the doublespeak which only causes ambiguity and confusion.

We read in Your word that You detest lying lips, but You delight in those who are truthful. God, as we sift through the endless claims and promises in the upcoming election, please move the campaign officials and marketing directors to address the public with truth.

Please enlighten our political candidates to the folly of making promises based on the shaky ground of polls and surveys. We need leaders who are unafraid to take clear stands on vague issues. We need leaders who stand on the solid ground of truth and who value character and honesty.

Amen.

Scripture references:

1 Samuel 16:7; Psalm 7:9;
Proverbs 12:22, 15:2 (CEV);
Matthew 12:34

MAKE A DIFFERENCE IN YOUR LOCAL NEWSPAPER

One of the most popular and well-read sections of a newspaper is the opinion section. This is where the general public can make their voice heard by writing a letter to the editor. Although newspapers in this country seldom include news articles from a Christian viewpoint, they may publish a well-written letter to the editor.

This is your opportunity to stand up and make a difference by influencing the opinions of others.

You can write a letter to your editor sharing your views on an important issue or to support a political candidate. Be clear and concise, brief and to the point, and try to keep your letter to less than 250 words.

STAND AND BE COUNTED
★ ★ ★

DID YOU KNOW?

S amuel Tilden won the popular election for President in 1876, but a handful of Electoral College voters from the State of Louisiana switched their votes at the last minute (this was a fall-out from the Civil War, and all kinds of bargains were being made politically), giving Rutherford Hayes the election by a mere single Electoral vote.

After removing Saul, he made David their king. He testified concerning him: "I have found David son of Jesse a man after my own heart; he will do everything I want him to do."

ACTS 13:22

A PRAYER FOR A PRESIDENT AFTER GOD'S OWN HEART

Almighty God,

Lord, as we enter into the upcoming Presidential election, we ask that You would give us a President who is a man after Your own heart.

Give us a President who will shepherd us with integrity and truth. May he be a man who places the

American people above himself. May he be a man of conviction who is more concerned about doing what is right than he is about securing a high approval rating.

Please lead us to a man who not only has deep-seated morals but is grounded in a relationship with You. May He seek direction from Your Word and from godly advisors. May he be a man of prayer who doesn't usurp Your authority but understands that he is answerable to You. And may he be a man courageous enough to walk in obedience to what You have required of Him.

Equip our President with the skills to lead the American people with knowledge and understanding. Give Him the wisdom to know how to bring the American people along with him as He follows after You.

Amen.

Scripture references:

1 Samuel 13:14, 16:7; 1 Kings 8:58;
2 Chronicles 16:9 (NASB); Psalm 78:72;
Isaiah 3:16; Jeremiah 3:15; Daniel 2:21

MAKE A DIFFERENCE WITH YOUR WALLET

You don't have to be rich to stand up and make a difference. You may be surprised to learn that most of the money raised by candidates is in small amounts: $25, $50, or $100—not large contributions. One recent candidate for President raised millions of dollars, all in small amounts.

Running a campaign is expensive. The costs to direct-mail, print yard signs, and produce and run radio and television advertisements can cost many thousands of dollars, even for small local elections.

STAND AND BE COUNTED
★ ★ ★

If you feel strongly about a candidate, contact campaign headquarters and ask how you can donate funds.

DID YOU KNOW?

In 1960, John F. Kennedy lost the popular vote to Richard Nixon by less than 100,000 votes. Nixon won the election based on the Electoral College. But in fact, the election was actually decided on a margin of less than 6,000 votes in the State of Illinois. Imagine the impact on America's history if Kennedy had not been elected President!

Religion that God our Father accepts as pure and faultless is this: to look after orphans and widows in their distress and to keep oneself from being polluted by the world.

JAMES 1:27

A PRAYER TO RESTORE GOD'S INFLUENCE IN OUR CULTURE

Dear Almighty God,

Not long ago our nation acknowledged You as the supreme authority of right and wrong, of good and evil, of righteousness and unrighteousness. We looked to You for guidance and relied upon your word for wisdom. And although we fell short, we still sought to anchor our country's moral underpinnings to You and Your word.

As those biblical supports are now being pulled out of the soil of American mores, we plead for Your intervention.

Please forgive us for refusing to acknowledge Your hand in our nation's affairs. "Every good and perfect gift is from above." You have blessed us and yet so often we turn our backs on You. Forgive our nation for exchanging the truth of God for a lie, and worshipping and serving created things rather than the Creator.

Move within our media outlets so they will tell of Your goodness and grace. Open our eyes and ears to identify Your truth that is revealed in our music, movies, and everyday events. At the same time extinguish the influences that run counter to Your holiness.

Through the election bring men and women to office who truly look to You for direction. May Your influence become greater and our influence lesser.

Amen.

Scripture references:

Isaiah 40:15; John 3:30;
Romans 1:25; James 1:17;
1 John 2:15-17

HOST YOUR OWN TOWNHALL MEETING

In early American history, candidates would travel from town to town to discuss their opinions and views in open forums with citizens, called "townhall meetings." Our country was founded on the discussions and decisions made in these meetings. Today, even with television and the internet, candidates like to engage in lively conversations with citizens.

If you want to get honest answers from political candidates, invite them into your own home. Contact a local candidate and tell him or her you are inviting a group of friends to a neighborhood coffee. Most candidates like to meet voters face-to-face and will probably gladly come into your home. Invite lots of people and make it worth the candidate's time.

DID YOU KNOW?

The closest election in Senate history was decided on September 16, 1975. The 1974 New Hampshire race for an open seat pitted Republican Louis Wyman against Democrat John Durkin. On Election Day, Wyman barely won with a margin of just 355 votes. A recount diminished the difference to just 10 votes, and in a new election demanded by Congress, Durkin won by 27,000 votes.

There are six things the LORD hates, seven that are detestable to him: haughty eyes, a lying tongue, hands that shed innocent blood, a heart that devises wicked schemes, feet that are quick to rush into evil, a false witness who pours out lies and a man who stirs up dissension among brothers.

PROVERBS 6:16-19

A PRAYER FOR PROTECTION AGAINST TERRORISM

Almighty God,

On September 11 the foundation upon which our nation's security and safety was based was shaken. We now realize we no longer live in relative isolation and security.

As we approach Election Day, please guard the United States from terrorist attack. Please place a hedge of protection around our President and political candidates during this dangerous season so that no foreign person or group will be able to influence the election.

Please guide our Department of Homeland Security as they work to foil any terrorist plans. Secure our borders so that no intent on destroying us will be able to enter. Give our customs officials extraordinary discernment so they will quickly identify any person or behavior that poses a legitimate threat to our nation's security. At the same time alert the Coast Guard to any suspicious activity that may uncover malicious plans of destruction.

Direct our foreign intelligence operatives so they will be able to uncover any plots for harming our country. Only You can join the nations of our world together to oppose and uncover these evil men. Show the leaders of predominately Muslim countries that these terrorists pose a threat to them as well. Open the eyes of any sympathetic nations so they will see these people as they really are.

Thank You that we can rest in the fact that when the earth and all its people quake, You are the one who hold its pillars firm. Your name is a strong tower; the righteous run to it and are safe.

May we, the American people, avoid empowering any terrorist or terrorist organization through our fear. Instead, infuse us with courage as we learn to lean on You.

Amen.

Scripture references:

Psalm 11:3; 75:3; Proverbs 18:10; Job 1:10

CONTACT YOUR CONGRESSMAN

The United States Congress is comprised of 435 Representatives and 100 Senators. These two bodies are important because they decide all of our laws, including how to tax and spend your money. How do they make their decisions? Usually their decisions are based on the views and opinions of their constituents—people just like you.

Here are ways for you to contact Congress about issues that concern you. You can visit the official web site of Congress at **www.house.gov** and **www.senate.gov**, or call 202-224-3121.

You can also visit **www.KnowWho.com** and for a small fee, you can download the e-mail address of every Senator and Congressman directly into your e-mail address book. Or you can visit **www.Congress.org** for complete lists and contact information for every member of Congress.

"These are the times that try men's souls. The summer soldier and the sunshine patriot will, in this crisis, shrink from the service of their country; but he that stands it now, deserves the love and thanks of man and woman."

—THOMAS PAINE

For he will command his angels concerning you to guard you in all your ways; they will lift you up in their hands, so that you will not strike your foot against a stone. You will tread upon the lion and the cobra; you will trample the great lion and the serpent.

PSALM 91:11-13

A PRAYER FOR THE MILITARY

Dear Almighty God,

You are a mighty warrior—You are strong in battle, skilled in combat, incisive in strategy and the victory always belongs to You. With You as our defender, we need not be afraid. Thank You for being our refuge and strength, an ever-present help in trouble.

With American troops stationed around the globe, we ask that You would draw our service men and women under the shelter of Your wings. Be their refuge, their strength, their ever-present help in trouble. Be their defender, encourager, confidant, and friend. Please use the perilousness of their vocation to drive them to a saving knowledge of Jesus Christ.

With so many scattered throughout the world, we need a President who will fiercely defend our troops. Please lead the voters to the man who will be conscientiously concerned about the welfare and protection of those who defend our country. Give him the wisdom to utilize our troops so they aren't exposed to unnecessary harm. May our Commander-in-Chief inspire courage and greatness among those who follow him.

Please protect our troops from harm. Encamp Your angels around them and shield them from danger. Open their eyes to any potential terrorist threats that may endanger them or others. Last of all, we pray for those Christians who serve among our troops. Encourage them in their walk with You and give them the strength to follow You in the face of temptation and ridicule. May their lives speak louder than their words and through them, may others find salvation in Jesus Christ.

Amen.

Scripture references:

Exodus 15:3; Psalm 46:1, 61:4;
Proverbs 21:31; Jeremiah 32:18

HOW TO RESEARCH THE ISSUES

In order to stand up and make a difference, it's important to become educated on the issues. But with so many books, web sites, and organizations, what's the best way to get started? How can you know who to trust?

Founded in 1973, The Heritage Foundation is a research and educational institute whose mission is to formulate and promote public policies based on the principles of our Founding Fathers. Their expert staff can help give you the tools you need to research the issues. To contact the Heritage Foundation, write 214 Massachusetts Ave NE, Washington DC 20002-4999, 202-546-4400, or visit their web site at **www.towhhall.com**.

STAND AND BE COUNTED

"The strongest of all governments is that which is most free."

—WILLIAM HENRY HARRISON

[Jehoshaphat] appointed judges in the land, in each of the fortified cities of Judah. He told them, "Consider carefully what you do, because you are not judging for man but for the LORD, who is with you whenever you give a verdict. Now let the fear of the LORD be upon you. Judge carefully, for with the LORD our God there is no injustice or partiality or bribery."

2 CHRONICLES 19:5-7

A PRAYER FOR JUDGES AND OUR JUDICIAL SYSTEM

Almighty God,

As we approach the coming election we understand the implications of electing men and women to office: these men and women will directly affect and approve the people who will judge on Your behalf.

Please guide the American voters to candidates who believe in the rule of law. May they be men and women who look to You as the impartial arbiter of justice.

Lead our elected officials to judges endowed with the wisdom that comes from heaven—wisdom that is pure, peace-loving, considerate, submissive, full of mercy and good fruit, impartial and sincere. Lead them to judges who love truth and choose life, and who understand that no decision or person is greater than the laws You have established through Your word.

We especially pray for our next President knowing that he will likely appoint judges to the bench of the Supreme Court. Guide us to the Presidential candidate who fears You more than the latest poll or approval rating.

May the words of the prophet Amos be fulfilled in our nation: "But let justice roll down like waters, and righteousness like an ever-flowing stream."

Amen.

Scripture references:

Numbers 23:19; Psalm 89:14;
Proverbs 29:4; Isaiah 30:18;
Daniel 4:37; Amos 5:24 (NRSV);
John 3:17; James 3:17

CHURCHES CAN STAND UP AND MAKE A DIFFERENCE TOO

Too often, churches think they can't make a difference in our democratic system. It is true that according to IRS regulations, a church should not endorse any political candidate or political party. Nor should a church distribute campaign literature, raise money for candidates, or do anything to persuade church-goers to vote a particular way.

But this does not mean churches should opt out of the American democratic system entirely. Churches can make a difference! A church can sponsor debates or forums, register voters, support get out the vote campaigns, and support issues in a non-partisan way. There are more than 300,000 churches in America. Imagine if each one tried just a little harder to make a difference.

STAND AND BE COUNTED

★ ★ ★

"Honest conviction is my courage."

—ANDREW JOHNSON

Then Elihu said: "Listen to me, you wise men. Pay attention, you who have knowledge. 'Just as the mouth tastes good food, the ear tests the words it hears.' So let us discern for ourselves what is right; let us learn together what is good.

JOB 34:1-4 NLT

A PRAYER FOR DISCERNING VOTERS

Lord Jesus,

During election time we, the voting public, are bombarded with messages and promises—many of which sound reasonable and truthful. But we're soon thrown into confusion when we hear contradicting messages and promises of others which also sound reasonable and truthful.

Jesus, we need ears to hear through the claims that solicit our vote. Because You are truth, we look to You to steer us through this confusion. By Your Spirit of truth, guide us through the messages of every candidate and issue. Please expose any hype or fraudulent claims that may lead us astray from Your truth.

Your paths are true and right, and righteous people live by walking in them. Give us eyes to see the paths of righteousness which lie before us. Make us aware of the stumbling blocks that lie hidden along the way. May we not judge by mere appearances, but make the right judgment. Most of all, transform our nation so we will become a righteous people.

You have made Your truth evident to everyone and Your wrath is vented against those who suppress it. We have no excuse for ignoring Your truth. Please open our eyes to the bondage that comes from self-deception.

Amen.

Scripture references:

Hosea 14:9 (NLT); John 7:24, 8:32, 14:6; Romans 1:18-19; 2 Thessalonians 2:9-11

SUPPORT A POLITICAL ACTION COMMITTEE (PAC)

Special interest groups form political action committees (PACs) so they can contribute money to candidates and parties. PACs have become very common and come in all shapes and sizes. They are formed by corporations, unions, or by groups of people who feel strongly about issues. When many small contributions are pooled together, they can be substantial enough to make a difference.

You can also start your own PAC with friends who share a similar view on an issue. Call 1-800-424-9530 for information. The Madison Project raises money for candidates who are pro-life and support pro-family, limited-government issues. They evaluate every Congressional and Senatorial race in America, and our endorsements are only extended to key competitive races which have a strong with the ability to win. Visit **www.MadisonProject.org**.

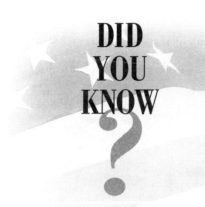

DID YOU KNOW?

When he was 23 years of age, Abraham Lincoln ran for the Illinois State Legislature and lost. When he was 29, Lincoln lost a battle for Speaker of the Illinois House. When he was 34, he ran for Congress and lost. When Lincoln was 39, he ran for Congress again and lost. When he was 46, he ran for the Senate and lost.

When he was 47, he ran for Vice President of the United States and lost. When Lincoln was 47 he again lost an attempt to be elected to the Senate. When he was 51, he was elected the 16th President of the United States.

"Now my heart is troubled, and what shall I say? 'Father, save me from this hour'? No, it was for this very reason I came to this hour. Father, glorify your name!" Then a voice came from heaven, "I have glorified it, and will glorify it again."

JOHN 12:27-29

GOD'S GLORY IN THE ELECTION

Dear Almighty God,

In this life, we will never be able to comprehend how loving, how merciful, how holy, how beautiful…how great…You are. All around us we see shadows of You. Shadows that point to the immensity of Your holiness and love. "The heavens declare the glory of God; the skies proclaim the work of his hands."

Since creation Your invisible qualities—Your eternal power and divine nature—have been clearly seen. Believer or unbeliever, none us is without excuse, and all of us will someday bow down at the feet of Jesus. Regardless of our acknowledgement of You in this life, this we know: You *will* glorify Your name.

Despite the inevitable, I *choose* to glorify Your name. More important than seeing my candidate or my cause win is seeing Your son Jesus lifted up. Regardless of the outcome of Election Day, I choose to give You praise.

Be glorified through our candidates, our ballot initiatives, the media. Open our eyes to see Your hand in the election and open the eyes of America to see the beauty of Jesus.

Our salvation comes from You—not from a political cause nor from any person. Even the random events and trivial occurrences find their beginning in You. So Lord God, I glorify You because You are the one who holds the universe together, who sets kings on their thrones and grants salvation to even the most undeserving.

Amen.

Scripture references:

1 Kings 10:9; Psalm 19:1, 24:7, 46:8-10, 86:9-10;
Proverbs 16:4; Matthew 5:16; John 12:32;
Romans 1:20; Philippians 2:9-11;
1 Corinthians 10:31; Revelation 7:9-10

STAND IN THE GAP FOR THE UNBORN

Over the last 30 years, more than 40 million unborn babies have been killed at the hands of abortionists. Help support key pro-life initiatives that include bans on cloning, research that destroys human embryos, the RU-486 abortion drug, and taxpayer support of Planned Parenthood (an organization that performed 227,385 abortions last year while referring only 1,963 women to adoption services). If you want to help, visit National Right to Life (NRLC) at **www.nrlc.org** or American Life League at **www.all.org**. You can stand up and make a difference by donating your time, money, or simply by becoming more educated on the issues that affect unborn children.

For you created my inmost being; you knit me together in my mother's womb. I praise you because I am fearfully and wonderfully made; your works are wonderful, I know that full well. My frame was not hidden from you when I was made in the secret place. When I was woven together in the depths of the earth, your eyes saw my unformed body. All the days ordained for me were written in your book before one of them came to be.

PSALM 139:13-16

A PRAYER FOR THE UNBORN

Almighty God,

The miracle of human life is beyond comprehension! How could you know me and love me before You even formed me in my mother's womb? Why would you choose to create me in Your image when You knew I would fall woefully short of Your holiness?

Heavenly Father, Your heart must break over the way we treat those whom You labored to create in Your image. Please forgive our nation for regarding human life as dispensable, disposable and cheap. Forgive us for mortgaging the lives of the unborn in order to safeguard the conveniences of the present. By suppressing the truth, we are invoking Your wrath.

Through the coming election we ask that You would bring to the leadership of our nation men and women of conscience. Men and women who fear You more than the prevailing opinions of our day, who understand that abortion is tantamount to murder.

Lord God please move in the hearts of the American people so they will understand that life is sacred and the right to take someone's life only belongs to You. Help our nation to see that by allowing abortion to continue we are really hurting ourselves: we're hardening our hearts toward you, we're destroying our ability to love, and we're heaping guilt upon ourselves that suffocates our souls.

Open our eyes to see that the abortion issue is a window into our hearts. Please renew our commitment to the sanctity of human life and draw us to the author of life—Jesus Christ.

Amen.

Scripture references:

Genesis 1:27; Psalm 139:13-16; Acts 3:15; Romans 1:18; Ephesians 3:18

CONTACT LOBBYISTS

Although the term "lobbyist" has no legal definition, it usually refers to someone who is paid to represent special interest groups. These are people and organizations dedicated to standing up to make a difference. There are pro-life lobbyists, anti-tax lobbyists, pro-family lobbyists and many others. Lobbyists know the intricacies of government inside and out and usually meet with legislators on a regular basis. They push for certain bills to be passed or form alliances with other groups to defeat a bill.

Legislators rely on lobbyists to help them make decisions on issues, because they know lobbyists represent large groups of voters. If you have a particular question or a strong opinion about a piece of legislation, contact a lobbyist. The National Association of Evangelicals (NAE) is a Christian organization in Washington D.C. the lobbies on behalf of Christian-oriented issues. For information, you can contact them at 202-789-1011 or visit **www.nae.net**.

SUPPORT THE FEDERAL MARRIAGE AMENDMENT

Marriage is facing a hostile attack in our nation. Lawyers and activist judges are engaged in a massive effort to re-define marriage for our entire society. If they win, the treasured values of family will be forever lost in our culture and children won't know what it's like to be raised in a traditional family.

If you want to get involved in the fight to save marriage and the family, you can support the Federal Marriage Amendment. For information, contact the Alliance for Marriage Foundation, write P.O. Box 2490, Merrifield, Virginia, 22116, or visit **www.allianceformarriage.org**. You can make a difference, but hurry because time is of the essence as activists are engaged in a hostile and hurried attack on the family.

STAND AND BE COUNTED

★ ★ ★

*"Our great resources...
are more especially to
be found in the virtue,
patriotism and intelligence
of our fellow-citizens."*

—JAMES MONROE

Everyone must submit himself to the governing authorities, for there is no authority except that which God has established. The authorities that exist have been established by God. For rulers hold no terror for those who do right, but for those who do wrong. Do you want to be free from fear of the one in authority? Then do what is right and he will commend you. For he is God's servant to do you good.

ROMANS 13:1, 3-4

A PRAYER FOR MORALITY IN OUR CULTURE

Almighty God,

Thank you that when our country was formed two centuries ago, You gave us founding fathers who believed in right and wrong. And although they weren't perfect, they understood the importance of a moral foundation based on the bedrock of Scripture and a belief in God.

God, at this time in our nation's history we need You to drive those moral anchors deeper. Keep us steadfast amidst the winds of amorality and immorality. Stir the hearts of the American people so they will know that You are the one true God, the God of righteousness and justice, the God who alone defines sin.

Forgive us for granting our sinful natures the license to run rampant. We have exchanged the truth of God for a lie, and worshipped and served created things rather than the Creator. Please renew within us the belief in absolutes that transcend individual preference.

Redirect our priorities toward whatever is true, noble, right, pure, lovely, admirable, excellent and praiseworthy.

Please bring to our leadership through the upcoming election men and women of virtue who value modesty over immodesty, purity over impurity, respect over tolerance, and integrity over corruption. Give us leaders who understand that the role of government is to punish those who do wrong and praise those who do right. Give us leaders endowed with the wisdom to know how to restrain sin without unduly controlling the American people.

Amen.

Scripture references:

Proverbs 14:34; Isaiah 30:18, 45:21; John 17:25; Romans 1:25; 1 Corinthians 3:11; Philippians 4:8; 1 Peter 2:14

CONTACT THE WHITE HOUSE

If you support or oppose the President of the United States on an issue, or if you want to let your voice be heard on an issue you feel the President should address, you can contact the White House directly.

Mail a letter to the White House:
    The White House
    1600 Pennsylvania Ave, NW
    Washington D.C. 20500

Call or fax the White House:
    Comments: 202-456-1111
    Switchboard: 202-456-1414
    Fax: 202-456-2461

E-mail the White House:
    president@whitehouse.gov

So when the crowd had gathered, Pilate asked them, "Which one do you want me to release to you: Barabbas, or Jesus who is called Christ?" For he knew it was out of envy that they had handed Jesus over to him. While Pilate was sitting on the judge's seat, his wife sent him this message: "Don't have anything to do with that innocent man, for I have suffered a great deal today in a dream because of him." But the chief priests and the elders persuaded the crowd to ask for Barabbas and to have Jesus executed.

MATTHEW 27:17-20

A PRAYER FOR HONEST ELECTIONS

Almighty God,

We read throughout Your Word that You defend the poor and oppressed. You are above bribery and You value the integrity of a person's word. You love honesty and detest corruption. You abhor dishonest scales—they are an abomination to You—but accurate weights are Your delight.

Safeguard any unsuspecting people against voting out of coercion or obligation to another person or group. Holy Spirit, we invite you to convict and prevent anyone from casting a vote that doesn't rightfully belong to them. Because you are a God of justice, our desire is that race, age, gender, education and income will not be a factor in who votes on Election Day.

Please give our governmental authorities keen eyes and discerning minds to detect voter fraud. Alert them to irregularities in our electronic voting systems and abnormalities in the way ballots are counted. We ask for You to place men and women impervious to corruption at our polling places to ensure that our votes aren't compromised.

Although honest elections preserve the fidelity of our democracy, we refuse to place our trust in the voting process. We place our hope in You knowing that You are the one who weeds out corruption and the one who ensures that honesty guides our election.

Amen.

Scripture references:

Deuteronomy 10:17; Psalm 25:21, 82:3-4; Proverbs 11:1,3; Isaiah 30:18; Amos 5:12; Matthew 5:37

BEST WEB SITES FOR CHRISTIAN VOTERS

With millions of web sites, how do you know how to become more educated on the issues, from a Christian perspective? We recommend the following web sites for news and current events from a Christian worldview:

www.WorldNetDaily.com
www.Townhall.com
www.FreeRepublic.com
www.ReligionToday.com
www.WorthyNews.com
www.Crosswalk.com

Each of these sites contains updated daily news, and in addition you can sign-up for free e-mail alerts.

Here is your part: Tell the truth. Be fair. Live at peace with everyone. Don't plot harm to others; don't swear that something is true when it isn't! How I hate all that sort of thing!" says the Lord.

ZECHARIAH 8:16-17 TLB

A PRAYER FOR FAIR AND BALANCED MEDIA

Almighty God:

During an election a great deal of the information we rely on to make decisions regarding candidates and issues comes from the media. We are at their mercy when getting our news. And because the media is composed of subjective people like me, I know that I cannot expect completely objective reporting.

Despite this fact, the media can be a vehicle which dispenses truth. Please set a guard over the voices of our newspapers, radio stations and television networks. Stir within our media an insatiable hunger for truth. We ask that You would reveal Your truth about the candidates and issues through the media and that they would become purveyors of Your truth without even realizing it.

Despite living in an increasingly secular society, which the media increasingly parallels, we also understand that they are not the enemy. We fight a much greater enemy: the devil, who hates truth and is the father of lies. Lord, we ask that You would shut the mouth of the Enemy so that he has no influence in the coming election.

Amen.

Scripture references:

Psalm 141:3; Proverbs 12:22;
John 8:44, 14:6; Acts 10:34;
Ephesians 4:29; 1 Timothy 5:21

CALL TALK RADIO

Talk radio has become one of the most influential mediums in American politics. Millions of listeners tune in to hear debates and to make their views known. If you want to make your voice heard, give talk radio hosts a call.

Make sure to call early in the show so you will be included in the program, write out your talking points to help you plan what you are going to say, and get to your point quickly when asked a question. You can contact local radio programs in your community or popular national hosts like:

Rush Limbaugh (1-800-282-2882),
Sean Hannity (800-941-7326),
Beverly LaHaye (1-800-527-9600),
or Janet Parshall (800) 343-9282.

"I believe in the American opportunity which puts the starry sky above every boy's head, and sets his foot upon a ladder which he may climb until his strength gives out."

—BENJAMIN HARRISON

For you have been called to live in freedom—not freedom to satisfy your sinful nature, but freedom to serve one another in love.

GALATIANS 5:13 NLT

A PRAYER OF THANKING GOD FOR FREEDOM

Almighty God,

Lord God, for more than 200 hundred years, men and women of faith and courage have laid down their lives to secure freedom for this country. Blood was shed—and continues to be shed—so that Americans can enjoy liberty, democracy, and the freedom to worship without fear of reprisal.

Because I am free I can choose between candidates and issues in the upcoming election, I can vote according to my conscience, and I can voice my opinion. Because I am free I can choose my profession and I can worship according to my convictions. Because I am free I can share the good news of freedom in Jesus Christ.

Thank you for allowing me to live in a country that makes it possible to follow Your divine call on my life. Thank you for instilling in the hearts and minds of our country's forefathers the importance of freedom.

When I consider times past and present, and countries near and far, I count myself blessed to live in the freest country of all. Thank you for allowing me to live in a country that is truly free.

As Americans continue in the footsteps of those who have gone before them, may we experience the freedom that comes from You. May we intuitively know the difference between liberty and license. May we use our freedom to serve one another in love. And may we yield to Jesus Christ, the giver of true freedom.

Amen.

Scripture references:

John 8:36; Romans 6:14, 8:1-3
2 Corinthians 3:17;
Colossians 1:13-14 (NLT);
1 Peter 2:16

STAND AND BE COUNTED

★ ★ ★

READ AMERICA'S FOUNDING DOCUMENTS

The original founding documents of the United States of America all include biblical language. This comes as a surprise to many Americans today. To help familiarize yourself with the true meaning and intent of our democracy, you should read the Declaration of Independence, the Constitution, Bill of Rights, Mayflower Compact, and even the Northwest Ordinance of 1787. To obtain these documents, visit your local library or contact WallBuilders, an organization dedicated to the restoration of America's founding principles. Call 800-873-2845 or visit **www.WallBuilders.com**.

STAND AND BE COUNTED

"Let us have faith that right makes might.... Having thus chosen our course...let us renew our trust in God and go forward without fear."

—ABRAHAM LINCOLN

This and other titles by White Stone Books
are available from your local bookstore.

Visit our website at:
www.whitestonebooks.com

*"...To him who overcomes I will give
some of the hidden manna to eat. And I
will give him a white stone, and on the
stone a new name written which no one
knows except him who receives it."*

REVELATION 2:17 NKJV